NATIONAL GEOGRAPHIC

Race to the Pole

Gare Thompson

Contents

Chapter 1

Antarctica

This is the story of a race between two explorers. Roald Amundsen and Robert Scott both wanted to be the first to reach the South Pole. To do this, they would have to overcome many dangers.

The South Pole lies near the center of the **continent** of Antarctica. This snow-covered continent is the coldest and the windiest place in the world. In winter, temperatures can fall lower than -120°F (-85°C). Howling, icy winds can knock you off your feet. **Icebergs**, huge chunks of floating ice, make the ocean waters dangerous for ships.

Amundsen and Scott did not let the dangers stop them. They were both ready for the race across over 1,500 miles (2,414 kilometers) of frozen land to the South Pole. Who would win?

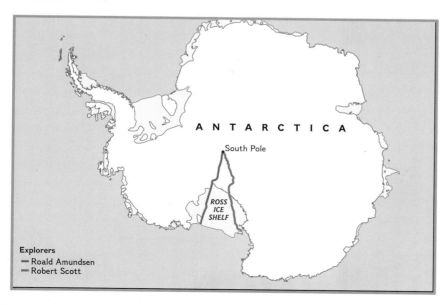

A N T A R C T I C A

South Pole

ROSS ICE SHELF

Explorers
— Roald Amundsen
— Robert Scott

Roald Amundsen

Roald Amundsen was born in 1872 near Oslo, Norway. Amundsen came from a family of sailors. At the age of 22, he began his adventures at sea. He became an experienced **polar** explorer. He explored the icy waters far north of Canada. On his sea voyages, he learned a lot about life in the Arctic. He saw how the native people dressed and what they ate to survive the extreme cold. He saw how they used dogsleds to get around.

In 1910, Amundsen set out for the North Pole aboard his ship the *Fram*. Then, he learned that two explorers had already reached the North Pole in 1909. So, Amundsen decided to sail to the South Pole. He knew that Scott was getting ready to set sail for the South Pole, too. Amundsen sent Scott a **telegram** telling him that he had changed his plans and was now on his way to the South Pole.

Robert Scott

Robert Scott was born in Plymouth, England, in 1868. From an early age, he wanted to go to sea. Scott joined the British Navy when he was 14. He trained to be a scientist. As an officer, he led different explorations of discovery. He had even explored parts of Antarctica before. He spent two long

winters in Antarctica on another trip. On this trip, Scott and his team had come closer to the South Pole than anyone had ever been.

Now, Scott wanted to return to Antarctica. He wanted to be the first to reach the South Pole.

Scott was ready to set sail from New Zealand when he got Amundsen's telegram. He was shocked. He had hoped no one else would try to reach the South Pole before him. Scott decided that he would stick to his plan. He would not let Amundsen shake him. The race was now on.

Chapter 3

They're Off!

Amundsen Lands on Antarctica

At first, Amundsen told no one of his change in plans. The crew aboard the *Fram* thought that they were going to the North Pole. On September 9, 1910, Amundsen stopped to get supplies for the trip to Antarctica. The crew now had fresh water and food for the race. They also had 97 sled dogs. The dogs would prove to be the most important thing that Amundsen brought on his trip.

Amundsen and his crew traveled to Antarctica on the *Fram*.

Finally, Amundsen asked the crew if they wanted to go with him to Antarctica. The men did and the ship sailed on. They arrived at the Ross Ice Shelf on January 14, 1911, and set up **base camp**. They would stay there for nine months.

Amundsen was organized. He had planned every detail of the trip. Over the next three weeks, the team moved tons of food from the ship to the camp. The men also set out food along the trail to the South Pole.

While waiting for spring and better weather, Amundsen and his men got ready for the trip. They skied and trained the dogs. They looked for ways to lighten the loads that the dogs would have to pull. This would help the dogs go faster.

Amundsen made sure the men ate well. It was important that they stay healthy and build up their strength. He did not send his men off to explore the area. He did not want them to get hurt or lost. He took no chances.

Scott Lands at Antarctica

Scott set sail from New Zealand on his ship the *Terra Nova*. A bad storm hit the ship on its trip to Antarctica. Some cargo was lost, but Scott sailed on. He landed at McMurdo Sound on January 3, 1911, and set up camp on the Ross Ice Shelf. Scott's camp was not as close to the South Pole as Amundsen's camp. Scott's camp was on the other side of the ice shelf.

Scott arrived with his crew, ponies, dogs, and gasoline-powered sleds. The men used the motor sleds to take the food and supplies to base camp. The first hint of danger came when one of the motor sleds fell through the ice and sank.

By the end of two weeks, the men had built a hut. They had a place to eat and sleep. Scott began to put food along the trail that they would take to the South Pole. They used the ponies and dogs to pull the food. The motor sleds did not work in the ice and snow. The ponies tired quickly and were hard to control. Unlike Amundsen's men, Scott's crew did not know how to use the dogs.

Scott and his men explored the area. At times, the men returned to camp tired, frostbitten, and cold. The dogs, tired and hungry, often fought each other.

Robert Scott
used ponies
to carry supplies.

Chapter 4 The Race

Amundsen Sets Off

Amundsen set off for the South Pole on October 20, 1911. It was a perfect day. The sky was beautiful and clear. The air was cold, but the men had dressed warmly. Amundsen and his crew of four set off with high hopes. They took four sleds piled high with supplies. Twelve dogs pulled each sled. The men had trained the dogs well. They listened to the men's commands.

The men made good time. On their first stop, the men found the supplies they had stored along the route. They fed the dogs **blubber**, or whale fat, and seal meat. The dogs hungrily ate their feast. The men ate their meal and slept.

Early the next day, the men left on skis. The dogs pulled the sleds. The men traveled about 13 miles (21 kilometers) per day. It took them about five hours to go that far. Then they stopped.

They built a small mound of stones. Inside the mound they put a record of the distance and direction to the next one. These mounds marked the trail. After building the mound, they ate and rested until the next day.

Amundsen and his crew set off for the Pole with sleds pulled by dogs.

Getting Closer

On November 11, they saw mountains. Amundsen named the mountains the Queen Maud's Range after the Queen of Norway. That night they camped at the foot of the mountains. They still had 340 miles (547 kilometers) to go.

The men and the dogs began the climb on November 18. Four days later, they were at the top. A howling **blizzard** set in that trapped them for four days. But the men could not waste time. For the next ten days, the men and 18 of the strongest dogs struggled against strong wind and fog. They fought their way across thin ice that covered deep pits. They kept going.

Finally, on December 8, the sun shone. The men were less than 100 miles (160 kilometers) from the South Pole. The dogs were hungry and tired. The men were sore and frostbitten. Their hands and faces were almost frozen. But they pushed on. Amundsen worried that Scott might have already beaten them.

Planting the Flag

On December 14, a cry of "Halt!" filled the air. Amundsen and his men had reached their goal. Each of the men placed a hand on the flag of Norway. They planted it together. Amundsen named the area King Haakon VII's Plateau after the King of Norway.

The men set up a tent. They took photographs and explored the area. They celebrated with a feast of seal meat. One of the men pulled out cigars. Inside the tent they left a letter for the King of Norway and a message for Scott. Amundsen had won the race!

Amundsen and his men planted the Norwegian flag at the South Pole.

Scott Sets Off

Scott set off for the South Pole on November 1, 1911. He traveled with a team of 10 men, 10 ponies, 23 dogs and 12 motor sleds. Scott had high hopes he would beat Amundsen.

Things went wrong almost at once. The weather seemed to be against Scott and his team. The men didn't have the right clothes. Several men became ill.

The motor sleds were useless. So were the ponies. The ponies sank deep into the snow and had trouble surviving the cold. But Scott was determined to make it to the South Pole.

First, Scott had to make it across the Ross Ice Shelf. Scott and his men marched there on foot. Some had skis, but it did not seem to help them. Scott's men were not used to skiing.

The men fought constant snowfalls. Temperatures never rose above 0°F (-32°C). It took them 15 days to reach the first stop where food had been stored.

Scott led the men onto the next stop. On December 5, the men woke to a fierce blizzard. The snowstorm forced them to stay put for four days. Their sleeping bags were wet. The men were tired and ill. On the fifth day, the men moved on. Two days later they had crossed the Ross Ice Shelf.

Scott sent the dogs and some of the men back to base camp. Now, the remaining men had to pull the sleds with their heavy **cargo**. The men sank into snow up to their knees. Their hands froze. But they struggled on.

Scott led his team across the ice towards the South Pole.

Reaching the Top

Finally, on December 20, the party reached the top of the **glacier**. Scott sent some of his men back to camp. He took four men with him to the Pole. The men grew weaker. It seemed as if every day they battled frostbite, harsh winds, and rugged land. They celebrated Christmas with a meal of chocolate, biscuits, meat, and candies.

By January 6, the party was far south. They saw no sign of Amundsen. They hoped that they were beating him. The next few days were hard. Another blizzard hit. Pulling their sleds now seemed harder. Scott knew his men were very tired, but he continued on.

On January 16, Scott and his team were very close to the Pole. They thought that they might reach it the next day. Suddenly one of Scott's men spotted a black speck. What was it? The men kept walking. Then they saw the remains of a camp. It was their worst fear. Amundsen had gotten to the Pole first. The black speck was his flag.

Finally, on January 17, 1912, Scott and his men arrived at the South Pole. A tent with a note from Amundsen was waiting for them. Amundsen asked Scott to get a letter to the King of Norway if he didn't make it back home. Amundsen also told Scott to use anything he and his men had left behind. Scott and his team were disappointed. On January 19, he and his men set off for base camp.

Scott and his team found Amundsen's tent waiting for them at the South Pole.

 # The Return Trip

Amundsen's Safe Trip Home

Amundsen and his men felt proud as they made their way home. They set out three days after planting the flag. It was a bright, sunny day. Amundsen seemed to have all the good weather and luck. Amundsen wanted to get back as fast as he could. He wanted to tell the world that he had been to the South Pole first.

He and his men quickly went back. They stopped for food at the mounds they had built on the way to the Pole. For most of the trip back, the weather was good. It was cold, but there were no blizzards or big storms.

The team made it back to camp in 39 days. All five men were healthy and happy. Amundsen took the ship back to Tasmania, Australia. The trip took a month. It seemed to take forever. Upon arriving, Amundsen immediately sent a telegram to his brother. Now the world knew that Amundsen was the first person to reach the South Pole. The *New York Times* reported that "the whole world has now been discovered."

Amundsen was given a gold medal for being the first person to reach the South Pole.

Scott's Last Trip

Scott and his men were tired and cold. They had very little food left and they had a long trip ahead of them. Scott was not sure if they could make it back to camp. He hoped the weather would be good.

The lack of food hurt the men. They became weaker and weaker. One man, Edgar Evans, fell on a glacier. He hurt his head. He tried to keep going, but he could not. His hands were frostbitten. He could not pull his sled. He died in his tent.

Now there were just four men. They struggled on. The men walked less and less each day. They tried to eat less, but they needed their strength. The weather worked against them. Storms hit. Temperatures fell well below freezing, even in the day.

Scott and the men trudged on. They grew weaker by the day. They needed food. On March 21, 1912, they were only 11 miles (18 kilometers) from a food stop. It would save their lives. But then a blizzard hit. It lasted for nine days. The men could not move. They died in their tent.

Eight months later a search party found the men. They also found Scott's journal. It tells the tale of their sad trip.

IN MEMORY OF THE
ANTARCTIC HEROES,
THE LATE CAPTAIN SCOTT
AND HIS GALLANT COMRADES,
WHO PERISHED
MARCH, 1912,
AT THE
SOUTH POLE.

Chapter 6 Antarctica Today

Today, scientists from all over the world live and work in Antarctica. They have set up large **stations**, which are like small towns. These stations have movie theaters, churches, banks, and hospitals.

The scientists study the weather. They observe the animals in the sea. They watch the ice to see how it changes. Helicopters carry supplies to the scientists who live there.

Tourists also visit Antarctica. They travel there to see what life is like on the frozen continent. Amundsen and Scott would be proud that the land that they explored still interests so many people.

Even though Antarctica is a frozen land, many animals live in the sea around it.

Glossary

base camp   the starting place or headquarters for an expedition

blizzard   a blinding snowstorm with very strong winds

blubber   whale fat

cargo   load of goods or supplies

continent   one of seven great areas of land on Earth

glacier   a large piece of ice that moves very slowly down a mountain or across land

iceberg   a large piece of ice floating in the sea

telegram   a message sent using a code of electrical symbols

polar   relating to the North or South Pole

station   place set up by a group for a specific purpose, such as studying the weather

Index